INSIGHTS

Actionable ideas
for business growth
and sustainability

DAVE GARDNER

Foreword by Rajesh Setty

"I look forward to Thank God Its Monday each week. Sometimes I cringe, sometimes I laugh and I always learn something."
— Joyce Mullen, President, Global Channel, OEM and IOT Solutions at Dell EMC

"I look forward to "Thank God Its Monday" to kick off my work week with keen industry insights and perspective that tap into Dave Gardner's vast expertise."
— Bobbi (Salata) Dangerfield, Retired Dell SVP, Global Business Services

"Dave Gardner's post is the one Monday email I can count on to help me think differently about the week ahead. An easy read that I often share with my team and colleagues to remind us about the bigger picture!"
— Amanda Hodges, Senior Vice President North American Marketing Dell EMC

"There are very few things I can honestly say I look forward to on Monday mornings, however, receiving my copy of "Thank God It's Monday "over the last 5 years, is definitely one of them. I find myself captivated and inspired with the content and how it relates to real life, every time, without fail. #CustomerExperience"
— Lisa Grimes, Chief Listening Officer | Customer Advocacy | Social Listening Intelligence | Strategist | Dell

"Thank God's It's Monday ... because lazy Sundays are overrated and get boring. I always need to get back to my Bring It On Mode ... whew, It's Monday!"
— Sue Chen, CEO, NOVA Medical Products, Shark Advocate, Hazelnut Farmer

"Mondays are better with 'Dave.' Always look forward to a new and enlightening, thought provoking, why didn't I think of that topic. Over the years, Dave has always gone, where for some never will...A straight-shooting, organized, thought-provoking topic in a chaotic business world."
— Daniel Howard, President, DJ's Scuba Locker Inc., www.djscuba.com

"Dave Gardner has a unique ability to take real-life examples from businesses large and small, from his own experiences in life, and from news stories, and then turn them into insightful observations that help people excel in business and in life. Several times, his insights have changed how I'm approaching specific challenges in my business."
— David Motto, Creator of the Ten Minute Virtuoso Method

"At a time when our inboxes are invariably clogged up with irrelevant, often useless "content" from a never-ending stream of experts, Dave Gardner's Thank God It's Monday is one of the few weekly mailings I read, respond to, and look to apply in my own business. Now Dave has compiled 100 of these short and insightful posts in book form. Ideal for those of us who want to have Dave's wit and wisdom at our fingertips across the five highly relevant business challenges in which he excels. If anyone can make the complex simple, he can. Here's the evidence."
— Dr. Liz Alexander, Thinker, Writer, Adventurer

"Honestly, I don't look forward to reading my email on Monday morning. But there is one exception, Dave Gardner's 'Thank God It's Monday' emails. I love his perspective and it makes me stop and think a bit versus just reacting."
— Greg Davoll, Senior Product Leader—Software Industry

Contents

Contents

Contents

Acknowledgments

I want to acknowledge several people who have had the greatest impact on my writing:

Jay Abraham, who taught me to write as though I was seated directly across from someone and sharing something they needed to hear. I learned to write to communicate, not write to impress.

Alan Weiss, my mentor, who has written some 60 books and who is a great exemplar writing as a craft. Alan is very succinct, a fabulous communicator and brings superior execution to everything he does.

Rajesh Setty, my friend and colleague, who suggested I create this book. Rajesh is the consummate entrepreneur.

I am grateful for my clients, who are a constant source of insights.

And, of course, I want to acknowledge my wife, Nancy, and my father, Robert, both of whom offer unending encouragement for my work.

Foreword

I have known Dave Gardner for a very long time, probably more than a decade. And I've also been a subscriber of his weekly newsletter, *"Thank God It's Monday"* for that entire time.

Starting from the title of his newsletter, everything that Dave does is extremely thoughtful. There is always take-home value from his newsletter.

One fine day when we were having coffee, I told Dave that he needs to get the value he creates weekly in the hands of more people. We brainstormed the concept for the book you have before you right now.

Sometimes, Dave would cover things that were topical (or relating to current events), but there would always be one or two insights packed within the newsletter. People who are long-term subscribers know that there is something they can take away, something they can share with their friends, family, or co-workers, and, most importantly, there is something actionable for the reader.

His insights range from business execution, customer experience, customer service, entrepreneurship, or innovation. There is a nugget of wisdom each week.

I'm delighted that Dave decided to package this information as a book because this represents the breadth of his life's work. What Dave has accomplished has helped companies fine-tune their execution machines so they can win in their marketplace.

You have in your hands a book that, while it looks like a small little book with 100 insights, is packed with the rich experience of several decades of Dave's experience helping clients improve and sustain business improvements long after he is gone.

This book is almost as though you have Dave to consult with you and your business, give his best insights packaged in 5 impactful sections, and, all for a small amount of money compared to what you would pay him for a day's consulting work. It's a steal that you are getting this wealth of knowledge packed, organized, and ready to be consumed and acted upon.

I wish Dave the very best of success with this book. I am so glad that he is finally bringing this to the world.

Rajesh Setty
Entrepreneur, Author, Teacher ,and Creator of the ThinkBook Series of books

rajeshsetty.com

How To Use This Book

Most executives and their team members are too busy being busy. There is never time for the important issues of the day, only the urgent issues of the day.

Executives and their teams don't take the time to stop and consider external ideas—they don't think they have the time. They ignore external ideas to their own detriment.

This book can be used in several ways:

• Some leaders take a particular section and lead a discussion with their teams. Most sections are intended to inspire discussion and action or offer a perspective that might be missed or overlooked.

• Some executives simply read these ideas as a source of inspiration for themselves.

Take time to ponder a specific topic and take action if appropriate.

The book is broken into sections:

• **Business Execution** is about getting things done, making things happen. The section is a great section to look at if you are trying to raise the bar or become unstuck.

• **Customer Experience** is about understanding your company from the customer's perspective. If things don't feel right to you, you can bet customers aren't impressed either.

• **Customer Service** really isn't a department—it's your mission as a company or as an individual to serve customers regardless of which functional area you are in.

• **Entrepreneurship** is about connecting with customers to ensure your venture is a success. At the end of the day, your idea—your dream—has to connect with the marketplace in a big way if you are to realize the success you crave.

• **Innovation** is about learning from what others have done that created excitement or were flops. I offer perspective to make your innovations relevant and valuable to your customers.

Here's the bottom line: if you continue to do things from the same perspective you've always had, it's unlikely you will break out in a new way. If just one idea in this book inspires you, it could bring you a new level of success.

Introduction

Each week I have the pleasure of writing a weekly missive to my email list that I call *"Thank God It's Monday." "Thank God It's Monday"* is a short, pithy piece intended to impart value, wisdom, an insight, or a perspective on the world of business.

It's my fervent hope that each time a reader sees *"Thank God It's Monday,"* they are encouraged to come back and read the next issue. It seems to be working as unsubscribes are extremely rare.

Some readers tell me they can't get to it every week and I certainly understand that. I simply ask that when you see the email—even if you don't open and read it— please think to yourself:

• How can Dave help me make the complex simple, or,
• Whom do I know that would benefit from Dave's work?

When I encounter readers as I go through life, I'm always delighted to hear stories of how much they enjoy receiving *"Thank God It's Monday"* each week and often hear that my writing has favorably moved them. That makes it worthwhile.

I started this in 2010 and plan to write it for many years ahead.

I hope you enjoy this compilation.
I'd love to hear from you.

BUSINESS
EXECUTION

1

Business Does Not Have To Be Complicated

Business does not have to be complicated, especially for companies that are thriving.

- Your capacity to get the things done that matter to customers is meeting the needs of and enhancing relationships with your customers.

- Your employees are excited and enthusiastic about coming to work.

- Your company's profitability is meeting or exceeding your expectations.

If one or more of these attributes do not characterize your business, you would be well-advised to identify and resolve impediments that are keeping your business from thriving.

Notes:

....

....

....

....

....

....

Winning During Market Transitions

While keeping your head down focused on your core business is critically important, leaders must raise their heads up occasionally to see how the world is changing and evolving to ensure continued marketplace viability for the owners, employees, and customers.

Companies that thrive lead and dominate during market transitions, e.g., Cisco Systems, Amazon. Companies in a death spiral, e.g., Blockbuster, Palm, et al., watch market transitions occur before their very eyes and later wonder how they could have missed the transition.

Notes:

....

....

....

....

....

....

3

It's All About Your Customer

Look at everything through the eyes of the customer; understand all customer experiences determine whether customers come back for more.

Using social media to identify customer satisfaction issues is good, but only if you relentlessly follow up to resolve customer issues.

If there is no closed-loop corrective action process, then the lesson you learn is of no benefit to your company or your customers.

Companies that thrive pro-actively head off issues before they create friction with customers.

Notes:

. . . .

. . . .

. . . .

. . . .

. . . .

. . . .

4

Continuous Improvement Is A Differentiator

Kaizen, a Japanese word for "improvement" or "change for the better," is an approach for eliminating waste and improving business execution.

Kaizen is not a program or a project with a beginning, middle, and an end—it is a never-ending quest to implement changes that ensure a company, a department or a function continues to improve.

How is your department eliminating waste and improving each month, quarter, and year to ensure you thrive?

Notes:

....

....

....

....

....

....

5

Your Business Through Your Customers' Eyes

Have you looked at the customer touch-points in your business through the eyes of your customers? Do you understand how your business works from their perspective?

Businesses that thrive understand it's all about the customer and do things that enhance relationships with customers, not leave customers shaking their heads.

Notes:

. . . .

. . . .

. . . .

. . . .

. . . .

. . . .

6

Eliminate Organization Gridlock

Gridlock is prevalent in our world: it dominates the news. It almost seems "normal."

Gridlock undermines progress on critical initiatives and impedes day-to-day business operations. Organizational gridlock often requires business process changes and, in some instances, new information technology.

The most significant contributor to organizational gridlock is a company's culture, which can be as toxic as the crude oil spewing from 5,000 below the surface of the Gulf of Mexico today.

Businesses that thrive do not tolerate gridlock, are consistently on the lookout for gridlock, and take quick action to quash it.

Notes:

....

....

....

....

....

....

....

7

Are You Perfecting Mediocrity?

A consulting colleague, Tom Taormina, was contemplating writing a yet unpublished book titled "Perfecting Mediocrity."

As I envision it merely from the proposed title, "perfecting mediocrity" is the dominant gravitational force for the vast majority of companies— good enough to survive but never great enough to thrive.

Is your company "perfecting mediocrity" or preparing to thrive? You know the answer. Are you ready to take action?

Notes:

....

....

....

....

....

....

8

Relentless Focus On Details Positions A Company For Success

From the terrific book *How to Castrate A Bull—Unexpected Lessons on Risk, Growth, and Success in Business* by Dave Hitz, Founder and Executive Vice President of NetApp, comes this gem about winning in business against a larger competitor:

"[The competitor's] key selling point was that their systems were faster, so that was where Brian attacked. He fixed every problem he could find. To motivate others to help, he awarded a bottle of wine to anyone who improved performance 1 percent. With each bottle, a little piece of [the competitor] died. One percent sounds small, but big improvements come in small increments, and Brian gave away many cases of wine."

The competitor Brian targeted, is no longer in business. His relentless focus on improving performance 1 percent at a time positioned his company to thrive.

What improvements are you working on to make your company, department, or team thrive?

Notes:

....

....

....

....

9

Work Ethic Is A Critical Component Of Success

Imagine waiting a lifetime for the opportunity to play professional football and having that opportunity end just days before the regular season begins.

22 players were recently cut from the San Francisco 49er's pre-season roster. Those who weren't cut had to breathe a huge sigh of relief: they had made it to the regular season. In a surprise move a couple of days later, the 49er's cut their third-string quarterback. Coach Singletary said:

"I really like the kid. There's a lot to like about him, but there's a work ethic that you have in terms of being a quarterback in the NFL."

Having talent but merely showing up doesn't cut it in the NFL or in any organization for that matter.

Companies that thrive know it's not enough to merely show up.

Notes:

....

....

....

....

....

....

10

You Can't Set It And Forget It

I had the good fortune of spending the weekend at a Kalispell, Montana, hotel that backed up to a very small airport. Just before dinner, my wife and I watched a gentleman in a small, single-engine Cessna practicing take-offs and landings as the sun set behind the mountains.

This reminded me that a pilot must maintain proficiency to keep his/her license current or face flying restrictions until issues are cleared.

Business execution is really no different. You can't assume that a process you put in place is relevant and works well today. To be effective, processes must be tested and validated for efficacy. If necessary, adjustments must be made to ensure the process business goals are achieved and maintained.

Companies that thrive are vigilant about ensuring their business processes and business execution meet high standards.

Notes:

....

....

....

....

....

....

Be Alert Today; Be Alive Tomorrow

Sign on Interstate Highway 80 near Elko, Nevada:

Be alert today
Be alive tomorrow

This warning works for business as well as driving. Constant vigilance will help your business thrive.

Notes:

....

....

....

....

....

....

Do You Only Have One Strategy For Success?

The plight of 33 Chilean miners trapped beneath 2200 feet of rock has captivated the world's attention since early August. The "Plan B" drilling operation succeeded in reaching the trapped men in just the past few days—nearly 2 months earlier than initially predicted. The "Plan A" and "Plan C" drilling veered off course and were abandoned.

When failure is not an option, we must applaud the Chileans for employing multiple, parallel approaches to rescue these men. I am grateful for the extraordinary efforts of everyone involved in this rescue. With great anticipation, I await the safe return of all 33 men to the surface in the next few days.

Recently, my "Thought for the Week" was:

"When obstacles arise, change your direction to reach your goal, not the decision to get there." -Zig Ziglar

The Chileans personify this thought.

Notes:

. . . .

. . . .

. . . .

. . . .

. . . .

Stuck Qi Harms People And Businesses

My superb traditional Chinese medicine acupuncturist and herbalist, Dr. Mark Wilson, helps me when I am ill. It is his job to identify and clear what we kiddingly refer to as "stuck qi (chee)," a blockage in an energy system or meridian impacting the health of the entire body. Boeing and Airbus might benefit from his services.

The new Boeing 787 test flights were on hold pending understanding why there was a fire in a power distribution unit. This is an example of "stuck qi"--the whole system is out of service until this problem is understood.

An Airbus 380 suffered a catastrophic failure of a Rolls-Royce engine shortly after take-off that, amazingly, did not result in the plane crashing. Until the design problem in the Rolls-Royce engine is identified and corrected; this is an example of "stuck qi." Some airlines prudently grounded their fleets while the investigation continues.

We see choke points or blockages in systems and processes all the time yet "learn to live with it." This is not a best practice.

Companies that thrive identify and clear potential blockages or choke points in systems and processes to ensure health. Unstick that qi!

Notes:

....

....

....

Why Enterprise I.T. Systems Are Needed

An enterprise information system must never be your raison d'être—your business is your raison d'être. You implement ERP, CRM, PLM ,and other enterprise information systems to improve your business execution.

If you fail to clearly identify your vision and the specific business outcomes ahead of starting an enterprise information system implementation, then it should come as no great surprise when your enterprise information system implementation misses the non-existent target.

To thrive, you must capture the essential business outcomes required for any enterprise information system before diving into implementation.

Notes:

....

....

....

....

....

....

15

The Captain Needs Feedback

A captain sees the world differently from the bridge than what the folks in the engine room see and experience. If you've ever felt that things at your company just aren't quite right, but you can't put your finger on what precisely those things are, then you're in the same boat (pardon the pun).

The problem is that when you occupy the lofty perch of senior management, you only receive filtered opinions and feedback from the people below you. That disconnect between you and the operating levels of the company undermines collaboration and business execution.

How can you overcome this problem? Get help from an independent third-party to assess your current situation to help you get the appropriate insights from the engine room to the bridge. This will help your company thrive.

Notes:

....

....

....

....

....

....

Are You Addressing Ineffective Processes?

Every business situation we encounter will either teach us about how things should be done or not done. There are lessons to be learned either way.

Too often, ineffective practices remain unaddressed as an issue is deemed too big a mess to tackle. This undermines a company, its employees, and, often, its customers.

Where are there ineffective processes in your company? Are you taking action to correct them?

Leaders must find a way to move the needle on ineffective processes. Acknowledge that all you need is success; perfection will always be elusive. This will help you and your company thrive.

Notes:

....

....

....

....

....

....

17

How We Are Rewarded

Paul Dunn shared the following insight at a seminar I attended in Australia back in 1994: *"We are rewarded to the extent we add value to other people's lives."*

I've never forgotten this, nor have I ever lost contact with this thought since. This is true for entrepreneurs, solopreneurs, businesses, and individuals.

What are the rewards? They can come in many forms: a simple thank you, financial or economic remuneration, the outcome related to good deeds, a referral, etc.

If you aren't happy with the rewards you or your company is receiving, one need only assess the value you are providing. How might this compelling thought help you and/or your company thrive?

Notes:

....

....

....

....

....

....

What Process Improvement Initiatives Should You Focus On?

One of my international colleagues mentioned that he encourages his clients to stop work on process improvement projects that don't impact business execution and the customer experience. I agree.

Process improvement projects must bring demonstrable value that moves the needle in a positive direction in terms of business outcomes. If you aren't sure about whether your team should be focusing on something, ask why they are doing it? You may have to ask why a number of times.

If you don't like the answer(s), direct your team to work on projects that favorably impact business execution and the customer experience to help your company thrive.

Notes:

....

....

....

....

....

....

You Can't Just Show Up To Thrive

As my wife and I returned from dinner last evening, we couldn't help noticing a 3-year girl skipping across the street in her bright pink shoes, pink leotard, and pink ballerina outfit. Her parents struggled to keep up with her excitement.

This young child offered a stark contrast with someone I met this past week about a job opportunity within a client company. The energy, passion, excitement of this person could not have been less in evidence. The person was going through the motions, giving me pat answers, and, apparently, looking for an opportunity to make some money, not engage with me about an exciting, start-up opportunity with a leading-edge technology division of a global company.

Showing up is not enough. Candidates need to demonstrate not only the capacity to do a job but also demonstrate initiative, passion, leadership in past roles, and enthusiasm for that role. It's these secondary qualities that help a person, and their company thrive.

Notes:

....

....

....

....

....

20

Proactive Action Is A Differentiator

Wei Yen, a well-known and highly-respected Silicon Valley software architect and entrepreneur offered the following insight back when he was with Silicon Graphics about resolving business process issues:

"Sometimes, when things are a bit broken, they need to become a little bit more broken before they can get fixed."

Customer pain doesn't have to be a catalyst to moving forward with solutions that are, often, all too obvious. Bad customer experiences open the door to the competition and market share loss. Proactively taking action to eliminate bad customer experiences will ensure your company thrives.

Notes:

....

....

....

....

....

....

Let Go Of What's Holding You Back

The movie "127 Hours" is a true story about outdoor adventurer Aron Ralston saving himself after a boulder crashes onto his arm and traps him in an isolated canyon in Utah. Since no one knew where he was, Aron faces certain death unless he can extricate himself from this seemingly impossible situation.

To live, Aron must amputate his trapped arm, climb a 65-foot wall and then hike 8 miles before he is rescued. Thankfully, he succeeded.

We are often trapped by situations that prevent us from moving forward unless and until we let go of what has been holding us back.

What do you need to let go of so you can thrive?

Notes:

....

....

....

....

....

....

22

Embrace The Status Quo At Your Own Peril

One of my consulting colleagues in Australia, Andrew Hollo, recently asked whether all organizations naturally experience growth, maturity, and, eventually, decline.

The answer is "yes" unless, of course, your company continually evolves to ensure relevancy in the marketplace. There aren't many buggy whip manufacturers today—the demand has dropped precipitously.

Eschew the status quo to ensure your company thrives!

Notes:

. . . .

. . . .

. . . .

. . . .

. . . .

. . . .

Being Purposeful Will Help You Thrive

As I headed to the office shortly before sunrise on a Saturday morning, I was greeted by a very long, white, jet contrail against a deep blue sky. I can't ever recall seeing such a long, perfectly-formed contrail. There were no winds aloft to erode the integrity of the contrail. The purpose and direction of the jet were not in doubt.

As I drove a few blocks further on this cool, crisp morning, I encountered a mother and her young daughter walking towards a hotel for an event. Both were moving at a fast, determined pace grinning from ear to ear as they set out for their day—you could see and feel their energy and excitement. Their purpose and direction were not in doubt.

After 30 years of authoritarian, dictatorial leadership, Egyptian protesters prevailed in a mere 18 days. If the Egyptian people don't ultimately get what they want, they'll be back in the streets. They are no longer victims—they have seized control of their destiny. The protesters left no doubt about their purpose and direction.

The signs are all around us. Companies and departments within companies that have a strong, purposeful direction (rather than an uncertain, meandering direction) will execute far better than those that don't. Embracing this understanding will help you and your company thrive.

Notes:

. . . .

. . . .

. . . .

FEAR: False Evidence That Appears Real

An executive coaching client continually gets caught up in FEAR: false evidence (that) appears real.

This individual sees problems that don't yet exist, sees parallels in situations that aren't parallel at all, imagines it's been months since the last contact from a prospect when it's only been a few days or a week or 2—all of which fosters a negative outlook about future desired outcomes.

What should one do in a situation where FEAR has taken hold? I recommend you ask the question, my mentor, Alan Weiss, asks: *"Where is the evidence?"*

Usually, when we look for the evidence, we pretty quickly determine that there really isn't any evidence at all—it's just FEAR rearing its ugly head.

Don't let FEAR keep you or your company from thriving.

Notes:

....

....

....

....

....

....

Business Must Collaborate With I.T.

I.T. is a critical enabler of businesses. There is, on occasion, friction between I.T. and business process owners about how to move forward to solve critical business challenges.

I recently interviewed four education Chief Information Officers in an effort to understand their culture and values and see if there is a contrast with what I have experienced in the private sector. Here are some best practices that will improve collaboration between I.T. and business teams:

• Business process owners would appreciate I.T. collaborating with them while working to minimize friction.

• Business process owners want I.T. to be part of the same team, not merely blocking and tackling the people who are responsible for day-to-day execution of a critical process.

• Business process owners want I.T. to get excited about solving real problems and spend a lot less energy pushing back on the business requirements.

• Business process owners want I.T. and their teams to win together.

If this culture of collaboration is engendered, everyone will thrive.

Notes:

. . . .

. . . .

. . . .

26

Current Growth Doesn't Portend Future Growth

A colleague offered that a client wanted to stop all consulting efforts as the business was growing rapidly, and everyone was moving at 120 miles per hour.

Respectfully, this isn't the time to disengage—this is the time to engage but engage in a way that is respectful of each person's time.

There are 3 key components to success: **people, process,** and **technology.** A breakdown in any of these can be quite injurious, particularly at 120 mph. None of these components were designed to work at 120 mph indefinitely.

A consultant can add value by watching for stress, making observations about the root cause, and by helping the team rapidly design and implement fixes to keep them moving at 120 mph.

When Diana Nyad swam from Cuba to the U.S. recently, she had a support team. She didn't leave the beach in Cuba and have everyone fly to the mainland to await her arrival. There were experts to help her every step of the way.

The most successful people and companies seek outside assistance to help them continue to thrive.

Notes:

....

....

....

27

Breaking From The Status Quo

The gravitational pull of the status quo is hard to break away from. Consider how much energy it takes to put a rocket into earth orbit...to break away from the status quo of the earth's gravity.

Change management is no different. You can't expect dramatic change to occur without a significant and sustained amount of energy and attention.

Understanding this will ensure your change initiative reaches earth orbit helping you and your company thrive.

Notes:

....

....

....

....

....

....

....

....

28

A Desk Is
A Dangerous
Place

John le Carré offered, *"A desk is a dangerous place from which to watch the world."*

Often, I.T. professionals are too separated from business process owners and the actual problems the business process owners are attempting to solve using information technology.

If more I.T. professionals would simply go to where the work is—watch and experience it first hand—they would be adding value beyond belief and helping their organizations achieve greater effectiveness.

This is how I.T. and Chief Information Officers can help their organizations thrive.

Notes:

....

....

....

....

....

....

....

Focus On Performance

Marissa Mayer, CEO of Yahoo!, offered the following thought via @ FortuneMagazine on Twitter:

We need employees to think about their execution and we need them to think about their performance. Not potential.

To me, this means employees are engaged in the business and see how what they do impacts customers and the customer experience.

- What kind of a "wow" employees are creating for themselves and their customers?
- Are they passionate, engaged, and excited? Fist bumps and high fives? Or, dead calm.
- Do they see themselves making a difference or simply manning a desk?
- Showing up for a paycheck or driven to do the best they can for themselves and their company?

If Steve Jobs left us anything, it has to be the notion that superior execution and creating a great customer experience is the key factor between surviving and thriving. This comes as a result of being intentional and conscious about everything you do.

Notes:

....

....

....

....

Threats To Your Security?

India is a powerhouse, emerging economy with a population of about 1.2 billion, comprising 17% of the earth's population of 7 billion people.

Last week, India's power outages impacted 700 million people in the northern portion of the country. As my father so aptly pointed out during dinner last week, 1/10th of the earth's population was without power.

Researching further, I came to understand that, on a daily basis, the region impacted by the power outages is only able to obtain about 92% of its power needs. Every day, people in the northern half of India wake, knowing there is a power shortage.

Infrastructure of all types is key to sustaining economic growth in India. Without constant infrastructure development, this region in India cannot thrive.

What infrastructure vulnerabilities does our nation have that are known yet little urgency exists to correct the problem? The I-35 bridge collapse in Minnesota in 2007 was actually identified as a risk back in 1990. Now, there is a multi-billion effort to repair Minnesota bridges that are 50% complete.

What threats are there to your economic security?

Notes:

. . . .

. . . .

. . . .

31

Tenacity And Focus: Key Success Factors

The National Geographic channel was live outside my office window Saturday morning in a show that lasted over an hour.

Up to four blackbirds teamed to chase away an overly-curious red-tailed hawk circling a nest in a large pine tree 50 feet from my window. The blackbirds dive-bombed the much larger hawk's body and its wings in a mid-air dogfight. At times, they were 30 feet above the ground and, at others times, probably 300 feet in the air. The tenacity of all the birds was admirable.

If only companies were as tenacious about dealing with potential threats to their well-being. The birds model a powerful process for dealing with threats: get on it and stay on it until the threat is removed no matter what it takes. This is instinctual.

Are your processes and commitment to dealing with issues that threaten profitable and sustainable growth as tenacious and effective? If so, it is likely you'll thrive. If not, you've got some work to do.

Notes:

....

....

....

....

....

32

Delighting And Exciting Customers

There are so many things that we take for granted:

- Being able to pay with a credit card
- A light coming on when we flip the switch
- Being able to flush a toilet and have running water to wash our hands
- Traffic signals never putting vehicles on a collision course
- Aircraft not colliding in the skies

Yet there are many things that don't happen as we had expected in our businesses:

- Delivering a fantastic customer experience across all touch-points in your business
- Getting new products into the marketplace on time that "wow" customers
- Deploying new IT systems on time and within budget that are widely and rapidly adopted by those who rely on those systems to get their work done
- Aligning resources with demand (people, inventory, supplies, etc.)
- Meeting financial goals for revenues and/or profitability
- Ensuring that people do what is expected of them--even when we aren't watching

The first grouping's success occurs as a result of superb business execution. The second grouping's success is far less predictable.

What actions do you and your business need to take to insure your business execution is as superb for the second grouping as the first?

Notes:

. . . .

. . . .

. . . .

33

Being Intentional

My wife and I had the pleasure of seeing the Spring 2012 art exhibition for The Academy of Art University in San Francisco--an institution founded by artists for artists in 1929.

Everything you would expect to see in a exhibition was there: paintings, photographs, pencil drawings of architectural concept drawings, interior design renderings, videos, animations, product labeling, web site design, sculptures, jewelry, clothing, etc. It was a remarkable collection.

The thing that struck me is how intentional everything is, how ubiquitous the things are in the collection, yet we tend to take everything for granted until we stop and take a closer look. There was genius in the work. Yet, outside the context of the show, we take much for granted, not realizing the enormous talent behind the final output.

How intentional is everything you do? The more intentional you are, the more likely you are to thrive and win as a few of these artists did.

Notes:

. . . .

. . . .

. . . .

. . . .

. . . .

. . . .

Turbocharging Your Business Execution

As a business owner or department head, you undoubtedly think you know about everything going on. And, for the most part, you probably have a pretty good handle on the essential matters. But do you know everything that you need to know? Probably not.

The best practice is to have an independent, third-party conduct an assessment to help you better understand where things stand.

- Your team members will say things to an independent third-party that they would be reluctant or hesitant to say to you.
- You'll get confirmation on things you may suspect are issues, and you'll likely learn some new things.

Whether your business has suffered a downturn and reduced headcount or you've grown in recent months or years, it's critical that you take some time to figure out where you stand.

Your team will really appreciate the opportunity to provide feedback. This is a significant, first step in turbocharging your business execution as it helps identify the logical and critical next-steps. This will help you and your company thrive.

Notes:

....

....

....

....

35

Want To Stay In Global 1000?

There is no better metaphor for business execution than the Olympics. The athletes work for years and years for a chance to, in a few brief moments, win a medal. Those who execute the best win--assuming, of course, the judges don't get in the way!

Imagine the thrill of being able to walk in the opening ceremony. That, by itself, is a tremendous victory. For many, the opening ceremony may be their greatest victory--only a tiny percentage of those who compete, win medals.

And, so it is in business. Out of all the companies in the world, only a few make it into the Global 1000. Some move into the Global 1000 each year as others fall out. Great strategy and superb execution ensure that a company gets in and stays in.

Just like the athletes, the great companies never stop looking for ways to evolve their strategy and improve their execution. Superb execution can help you, and your company thrive.

Notes:

....

....

....

....

....

36

3 Things General Electric's CEO Learned In The Military

Speaking at Dreamforce 2012 in San Francisco, Jeff Immelt, GE Chairman and CEO, offered 3 key things he's learned from military:

Be purposeful

Always work on what's important

Adaptability

These 3 things will help you and your company thrive.

Notes:

37

The Unlived Life

One of my favorite books is *The War of Art* by Steven Pressfield, a book about breaking through blocks in our life and winning our inner creative battles. I recommended it to a colleague this past week and grabbed it to read on the train to and from San Francisco. Here's an excerpt from a section titled "The Unlived Life:"

"Most of us have two lives. The life we live, and the unlived life within us. Between the two stands Resistance....

Resistance is the most toxic force on the planet. It is the root of more unhappiness than poverty, disease and erectile dysfunction. To yield to Resistance deforms our spirit. It stunts us and makes us less than we were born to be. If you believe in God (and I do) you must declare Resistance evil, for it prevents us from achieving the life God intended when He endowed each of us with our own unique genius."

Buy this book. Read this book. It will help you thrive.

Notes:

. . . .

. . . .

. . . .

. . . .

. . . .

38

Hunkering Down Is A Failed Strategy

HP has done what a lot of companies have been doing the past 3 years: hunkered down trying to ride out the economic downturn focused primarily on reducing costs while searching for sales.

HP has paid a price for this. And, so have other companies that have adopted similar strategies.

Defining and executing a compelling strategy, addressing critical business processes and system needs, and driving innovation is key to maintaining the vitality of a corporation.

There's no time like the present to tackle those issues you know are going to hurt your company as the economy continues to rebound. Take action to ensure you and your company thrives.

Notes:

....

....

....

....

....

....

Lessons Learned From Costa Concordia

The Italian cruise ship Costa Concordia disaster reminds us that, too often, we become cavalier about critically important things. Problems seldom materialize, so we become complacent. *"It won't happen to us. This is just another routine flight or cruise or trip to the grocery store--it's been done uneventfully thousands of times."*

After the cruise ship struck a reef this weekend, survivors report that there was utter chaos on the ship. News reports state:

- The passengers had not been briefed on what to do--the passenger safety briefing was scheduled for the second day at sea.
- The crew was ill-prepared to assist the passengers during this disaster and did not provide leadership at a time when it was needed most.
- It was reported a crew member did not know how to operate the life boat once it was in the water; a passenger took control of the vessel to get it to land.

We see business execution failures that should have prevented an accident in the first place being compounded by delayed disaster drills in the event of a need to evacuate the ship. Failure in these preventative measures created breakdowns in the contingent action: ship evacuation after the incident.

Had the crew ever done more than a chalk talk about what to do? Had they ever done full dress rehearsal? It doesn't appear so. And, the result is that even though there are few casualties and deaths, this lack of preparation undermined the experience for all concerned.

Luck is not a preventative or contingent measure. Luck may occasionally work well in gambling, but it won't consistently help you thrive. And, it certainly won't improve business execution.

Notes:

....

....

Growing Pains

In the business world, "growing pains" describes inefficiencies that creep into a business over time until such a point when the cumulative effects are debilitating.

During the past 4 years, many businesses have downsized and, due to revenue declines and limited budgets, needed action to optimize their systems and processes around new, lower revenue levels, and lower staffing levels has been deferred.

These companies are doing more with fewer resources with great pain, pretty much driving those who remain at the company nuts. The employees are chronically overtaxed, highly stressed, and waiting to flee the company in search of a new opportunity just as soon as they can.

A business is more than what it does. For a business to be "in business," it must have systems and processes that eliminate people dependencies and allow new people to join the organization and make a positive impact in short order. This allows for greater agility and speed. It allows for growth or contraction.

Does a business have to be brought to its knees from a business execution standpoint before action can be taken? Absolutely not. My best clients proactively engage with me to look at these issues.

Notes:

....

....

....

....

Do Headcount Reductions Make A Company More Competitive?

HP will soon be reducing its workforce by about 10%--30,000 people. President and CEO Meg Whitman signaled this possibility back when she discussed HP's fourth quarter results.

Cutting 10% of HP's workforce reduces expenses and sends a message to the those employees who remain that the status quo won't prevail. But, so what? The bigger challenge for HP is ambition, drive, and culture. What is HP leadership doing to:

• Create a lean, agile, entrepreneurial workforce, and culture?
• Create a less entitled workforce?
• Drive innovation that captivates customers and investors?
• Ensure it isn't a "me too" company?
• Build trust and respect lost with its employees lost over the past decade?

Ask yourself the questions above in the context of your company. What are you and your company doing to ensure you thrive?

Notes:

....

....

....

....

....

....

Changing How Work Gets Done

We often hear that a company is implementing an ERP, CRM, PLM ,or a product configurator system. Yet, by these very words, there is a lack of appreciation of what is really occurring:

You aren't implementing an information technology system; you are changing the way work gets done.

By itself, information technology accomplishes nothing. Leverage comes from the integration of people and process with information technology. Most projects focus too much attention on the technology and too little on people and process.

A successful project must be a collaboration between the business team (the people who end up living with the efficacy of the business application) and the I.T. team. The joint mission is delivering an application that enables the business team to accomplish its essential mission with greater efficiency and execution control.

Business teams must actively engage with I.T.--their future relies on it. Only through active engagement will the business teams thrive.

Notes:

Being A Customizer Does Not Create Efficiencies

Being a "customizer" doesn't create efficiencies. More often than not, customization brings tremendous inefficiencies in sales, order administration, engineering, manufacturing operations, service, etc.

• You require significant human intervention to accommodate complexity and variety simply because the information isn't available--the business isn't set up properly.

• Your team is challenged to pull together quotes for products and services that can actually be delivered.

• Your team is challenged by the fact that nothing is standard; everything is a special.

Companies must evolve their business processes to cost-effectively meet the challenges product and service complexity brings. If customizers don't take action to improve efficiencies, they will continue to suffer margin and operational challenges that only mount. Failure to address these challenges will keep you and your company from thriving.

Notes:

....

....

....

....

....

CUSTOMER
EXPERIENCE

44

It's All About Your Customer

Mike Dreyer, CIO of VISA Inc., has been quoted as saying he doesn't want technology to be a limiting factor in implementing any good idea. A wonderfully refreshing thought!

Too often, people reject ideas that would better serve customers with weak rationales: "that won't work here," "that's not how we do it here," "it's too hard to do that," "we've never done that before," and my personal favorite, "the system can't handle it."

Is your company artificially constraining customer choice? Or, are you, like Mike Dreyer, taking the lead to make sure that good ideas find their way to the top so you can delight your customers and help your company thrive?

Notes:

....

....

....

....

....

....

45

Are Your Customers In The Driver's Seat

Back in 1961, Hertz ran a very memorable ad campaign built around a compelling theme: "Let Hertz put you in the driver's seat." As a tag line, this was powerful. Not only did it create the image of a customer ending up in one of Hertz's rental cars, it suggested that Hertz puts the customer in control of the relationship.

What could be better than a customer driving the relationship? Perhaps this simple ad set the stage for Hertz being the world's largest car rental company today.

How is your company putting customers in the driver's seat so your company can thrive?

Notes:

....

....

....

....

....

....

How Social Media Can Improve Customer Experience

Traditionally, when humans have experienced a less-than-satisfying experience, they often believed that there was no point in complaining— no one cares. Today, complaining about customer experiences is easier than ever, thanks to forums, blogs, and social media (Twitter, Facebook, LinkedIn, etc.).

If you aren't happy, you no longer have to suffer in silence—you can broadcast your disdain to the entire world using social media. Delighted or satisfied customers tend not to broadcast their feelings with the same frequency and passion—a sad fact of life.

Companies that thrive will look to social media to help them understand what the world is saying about them, so corrective action can be taken.

Notes:

....

....

....

....

....

....

Stop Saying, "I'm Sorry"

"I'm sorry" sounds so hollow, so ubiquitous, and so incredibly easy to say that I am growing weary of hearing it. Companies need to put some action behind their business execution challenges.

If your process breaks down and a customer has an experience that is less than what they deserve, tell us what you are going to do to make sure no other customer is inconvenienced in the same way. Let dissatisfied customers know that you are going to do something to create a better experience for them and all others who touch that process.

That's what customers want and need to hear if your company is to thrive!

Notes:

....

....

....

....

....

....

48

This Business Never Connected With Marketplace

The Friday before Thanksgiving, the Carl's Jr. fast-food burger emporium across the street from my office closed for business. There is nothing sadder than a business closing and the jobs lost, particularly at this time of year. Why did this happen?

- The staff could barely speak English. Sure, they could take an order, but most could not greet you properly, handle a conversation about special food preparation requirements, etc.
- A cook soon became a front counter order taker, whether they were prepared for or well-suited for this position or not.
- A customer was treated with indifference.
- You could see the fear in their eyes of many of the staff dealing with a non-Spanish speaking customer.
- The manager hired people just like him--there was no diversity in one of the most diverse employment areas you can imagine.
- The food was haphazardly and inconsistently prepared, e.g., the french fries were often lukewarm, a burger often had a huge clump of lettuce crammed between the meat and the top bun, etc.

Across the parking lot, the McDonald's thrives. Carl's Jr. has the potential for much better food than McDonald's, yet this location struggled for years. It's no wonder they closed, given the customer experience they delivered. Corporate seemingly didn't understand what they needed to do to make this location succeed.

Is your company delivering the customer experience that ensures it and you will thrive?

Notes:

. . . .

. . . .

Get Rid Of Gatekeepers

I reached out to the head of HR at the Four Seasons to understand how they are able to deploy such a remarkable team and provide such an incredible customer experience time and time again. *[Note: As I didn't tell the head of HR that I was interviewing her for an article (because I wasn't), I'm not going to share the details of my conversation.]*

However, I do want to share what happened as, it too, illustrates how the Four Seasons is able to create such a remarkable customer experience.

- I called the hotel and simply asked to speak with the head of HR. I was informed of her name and immediately transferred.
- When a woman answered the phone, I simply told her my name, that I was a management consultant, and informed her who I wanted to speak with. Her response was something like, "One moment please," and I was immediately transferred. I wasn't interrogated about why I was calling. No blocking, no tackling, no running interference. I didn't have to leave my phone number for a call back later. My request was fulfilled on the spot.
- The woman I was transferred to answered her phone, and we had an absolutely delightful, no-holds-barred conversation. I didn't get her voice mail and the ensuing opportunity to leave a message--I got right through.

How often does this happen in today's business world? Almost never. It is so refreshing that I feel compelled to write about it. I want to compliment the Four Seasons for superb execution on something this simple. It could have taken days to accomplish what transpired in seconds. But it didn't. And, the Four Seasons has created another "Wow" for me.

Are you and your company this easy to do business with? If you are, rest assured you'll be a stand out in your marketplace. And, if you're not, you'll stand out for all the wrong reasons.

Notes:

. . . .

. . . .

50

Earning Customers— Customer Choice

A Colorado colleague contacted me for a referral to a new stockbroker. His broker had left the firm, and he'd been assigned to someone in Utah. It was clear, he really wanted to deal with someone local.

I suggested he go to his brokerage office, speak the general manager, and ask to interview his top 3 brokers to decide who will handle his account.

It's easy for some companies to forget that they are dealing with customers who have a choice. If the firm handles this well from this point on, this relationship will be saved, and everyone will thrive.

Notes:

....

....

....

....

....

....

The Yum/Yuck Test

When a customer thinks about a company, his/her mind rapidly converges on a relatively few possible opinions about the brand:

- Yum--they like and are drawn to the company
- Yuck-they dislike and are turned off by the company
- No reaction--they haven't formed an opinion, either positive or negative, about the company

If your company is a "yum," you're in a very good place. If your company is neutral or has no opinion, you still have an opportunity to convert people to a "yum." If your company is a "yuck," you may have lost an opportunity to work with that customer again, particularly if there are alternative choices in the marketplace.

How do customers rate your company? If you aren't striving for a "yum," your company can't possibly thrive.

Notes:

....

....

....

....

....

52

When Customer Experience Is Not What It Should Be

A colleague reports that, after hosting a session about the customer experience, some employees reported being "uncomfortable" with what they heard. My, oh my.

It can be eye-opening to look at things from a customer's perspective. I recall Dell senior managers being a bit aghast at stories they heard from real customers when they hosted their first customer advisory panel meeting a few years ago. It hurt, but they took action. And, Dell is a better company for having started the dialog and following through to close the gaps.

It's okay for employees to be uncomfortable if it brings the perspective needed to help them interact more effectively with customers. It's not okay to ignore what you're hearing.

It's what you do with the insights or perspectives you gain about your customer's experiences that can help your company thrive.

Notes:

....

....

....

....

....

53

Customer Experience Is Viewed Holistically By Customers

It is easy to add up the pluses and minuses of the complete experience we personally have with a company to help us decide if we will be a repeat customer.

Why is it then, when we are inside a company, negative customer experiences emanating from touch-points in different organizational silos seem to be less important to the company? Why do we tend to believe that (from the safety of our silos) that the customer will only remember the positives and forget about any negatives?

I know of a fire/rescue vehicle manufacturer where 90% of its deliveries were late by weeks or months to customer expectations. If a truck was being purchased for a new firehouse, how did the fire chief feel if that truck was not available to support the firehouse opening? Not good. Did all the other things that the company did right matter? No. That company now ships about 50% of the volume it once did. The fire chiefs did not forget.

Customer experience must be viewed holistically across the enterprise. Looking at the customer holistically will help your company thrive.

Notes:

....

....

....

....

CUSTOMER
SERVICE

Customer Service Is A Mindset, Not A Department

Just what is customer service? Some would say it's a department. I say it's a mindset that thriving companies adopt: they are in business to serve their customers. Why?

Anything and everything that impacts a customer and ultimately contributes to the customer's experience is, in effect, customer service. Sales, order administration, product development, operations, and the customer service organization collectively determine how the customer ultimately feels about the company, something referred to as the "customer experience."

Companies that thrive realize that they are in business to service customers and examine each aspect of the business to ensure that customers receive a great experience.

Notes:

....

....

....

....

....

....

55

Never Pretend You Care About Customers

What would you say about a company that offers support forums to its partners but then doesn't respond to problems? Is it really a support forum?

A company isn't in a partnership if it doesn't respond to partner requests for help--it enjoys a one-sided relationship, not a partnership.

The question that arises is whether the support forums are working as designed? If they are, this behavior is shameful. If they aren't working as designed, then managers who should be accountable aren't doing their job.

- A company provides voice mail as a vehicle to leave messages with the expectation that calls will be returned.

- A company provides email as a way to have bi-directional communication.

- And, a company should provide a support forum only if it is an avenue to get assistance with problems.

Companies that thrive treat customers and partners like gold. Companies that treat customers with indifference risk becoming irrelevant no matter how good or big they are today.

Notes:

....

....

....

56

Customer Service Trends You Need To Be Aware Of

I was invited to attend a Customer Service Think Tank hosted by Dell in Austin, Texas. Customer service experts and industry thought leaders gathered to ponder the challenges, opportunities, and future of customer service and support. One session looked at "the future of service:"

• Customer service will be at the core of what successful companies do-- it won't be an afterthought.

• There will be a lot less customer service as the most effective service is the call the customer never has to make as products get better and better.

• There's auto-detection of possible issues based on customer profiles and a known solution to problems. Other customers will benefit, as well.

• Smart semantics and artificial intelligence will help customer service personnel and customers converge on solutions faster and with greater ease--complexity will be less obvious to customers.

• Companies will become more community-driven--the community will be where issues and opportunities surface.

Are these ideas on your company roadmap? If not, how do you expect to thrive?

Notes:

....

....

....

Customer Service Technical Support Best Practices

I've had a terrific customer experience with everyone I have worked with at Verizon Wireless, going back to 2004. The products, services, and people have been great. I never cringe at the thought of interacting with this company. That's not to say they can't get better!

Here are my recommendations for improving the customer experience relative to a technical problem I've been chasing for a few weeks:

- Never close a trouble ticket without confirming with the customer that the problem is resolved via the proposed solution. More than one ticket was closed when I still had the same problem meaning no one was working on it!
- When you tell a customer you are going to call them back, call them back. Not hard. Yet, 3 different people promised to call me back and didn't.
- Never transfer a customer to one of your supplier's technical support organizations without (a) informing the customer that that is what you are going to do, and (b) getting the customer's permission. It's quite a shock to suddenly find out you aren't dealing with Verizon Wireless in the middle of a long call.
- When departments that need to be working together to get to the bottom of an issue aren't collaborating, escalate the issue within your organization to management and senior management to get them talking. It's not okay for an organization to be unapproachable when it comes to dealing with a customer issue.

Do these things, and I'll be a happier customer. If you have a customer service organization, avoid the mistakes I've identified above and, you and your customers will thrive.

Notes:

....

....

58

Does Your Company Have Big Ears?

How big are your company's ears? Is your company listening to what's being said in the world of social media? Can your company afford not to?

Verizon Wireless announced last week that it was going to charge a $2 per transaction "convenience fee" for paying a monthly bill via your phone, on Verizon's website, or via credit card/debit card not set up on a automatic payment basis. They would waive the fee for paying in Verizon store or via check. And, who was this deemed "convenient for?" I tweeted:

I love Verizon Wireless but $2 to pay my bill online or via my phone? This is insane. Do you think you're BofA?

I wasn't alone. Verizon heard loud and clear via thousands of social media messages that this "convenience fee" was dead on arrival with its customers. Charging a customer to pay their bill? Come on. Verizon--it appears you can hear us now, and you wisely reversed course 24 hours later.

But you don't have to be a Verizon-size corporation to leverage social media. All companies that thrive have big ears.

Notes:

....

....

....

....

ENTREPRENEURSHIP

You Never Step Into The Same River Twice

I'm a huge fan of Sir Richard Branson. Not only is he the consummate entrepreneur and leader of the Virgin Group of companies, he also knows how to have fun and create excitement. From his book "Business Stripped Bare," he writes:

"Every business, like every painting, operates under its own rules. There are many ways to run a successful company. What works once may never work again. What everyone tells you to do many just work, once. There are no rules. You learn by doing, and falling over, and it's because you fall over that you learn to save yourself from falling over...

Most of what I have done with the Virgin Group is about my own gut instinct. I've never analyzed what I do in any formal way. What would be the point? In business, as in life, you never step into the same river twice."

Sir Richard Branson knows how to make businesses thrive.

Notes:

. . . .

. . . .

. . . .

. . . .

. . . .

. . . .

Fall In Love With Your Customer, Not Your Technology

I attended DEMO Fall 2010 this past week, a show where aspiring entrepreneurs pay nearly $20,000 in registration fees to get a small booth and time on stage to present their innovation to analysts and firms looking for great ideas to invest in.

Chris O'Brien summed up my reaction to DEMO's entrepreneurs in his San Jose Mercury News article titled, *"What startups should focus on:"*

"I am constantly impressed by the crazy amount of energy entrepreneurs spend hatching innovative services, so I have never understood why they seem to spend so little time figuring out their business models. Most end up banking on their ability to sell ads to pay the bills and make money. Everyone convinces themselves that they will be the one startup to break out of the pack and make this work. But, this ignores the fact that no matter how much advertising shifts to the Web, there isn't enough to support even a tiny fraction of these startups."

One would have thought the dot com bust a decade ago would have etched Chris's insight in every entrepreneur's mind. If you believe that, you'd be wrong. I concur with his assessment. I asked many firms, "how do you make money at this", and most responded, "we're still working on the details."

Companies that thrive are enamored with their customers, not merely their innovation ideas. If it won't work for customers, it won't work for investors who provide the fuel ($$) required to launch and sustain a company.

Notes:

. . . .

. . . .

The U.S. Needs To Rekindle Its Mojo

New companies don't carry the burden of legacy baggage and sacred cows to the marketplace. They start anew, correcting, and improving upon what has come before.

For example, Boeing didn't expect upstart Airbus to eventually win 50% of its market share. Airbus, through a common cockpit user interface, made it simpler to train and move cockpit crews from one aircraft to another. The result is airlines using their aircraft are more agile and can expand faster.

China and India are hungry to participate and even dominate in the global economy—it's their omnipresent, burning desire. These countries are operating in the fast lane while the U.S. appears flat-footed and bogged down in complacency and indecision. While China and India aren't executing the strategy perfectly, they've not lost sight of the target either.

We need to re-kindle our burning desire, offer incentives to create jobs here in America, create disincentives for outsourcing jobs overseas that are not part of a legitimate global growth strategy, and not idly sit by and watch jobs that should be based here be exported overseas.

America's strength is its ability to innovate. Innovation will stimulate job creation and growth here in America.

The U.S. needs to get its mojo back—re-kindle our burning desire—if we are to thrive in the 21st century and beyond.

Notes:

....

....

....

....

How Entrepreneurs Thrive

I joined 20 entrepreneurs over a long weekend to deeply understand the path each has been on during their lives. Here's what I heard about the essence of entrepreneurship:

• It's about having an indomitable spirit, resiliency, resolve, and unwillingness to accept any obstacles thrown up in life.

• It's about the support systems, including our families, that make it possible to do what we do.

• And, finally, it's about connecting with people in a very authentic way.

Sound easy? It's not. This is what helps entrepreneurs thrive.

Notes:

....

....

....

....

....

....

Your Customers Are Intolerant Of "One-Size-Fits-All" Solutions

There are few things based on absolutes. Most principles exist on a continuum. People with food allergies have varying degrees of adverse stimulus response to the same allergen. Customized, configurable products and services are no different--they, too, exist on a continuum.

Not every product or service has to be a 10 in terms of feature or option quantity or complexity to be successful in the marketplace. Providers of configurable products and services are in charge of setting and managing their own continuum.

The decision made today about how configurable to be doesn't have to be set in stone. The continuum can change as the market changes and evolves or as your capabilities and ability to manage and offer configurability evolve.

Configurable product and service providers already know that they aren't in a "one-size-fits-all" world. It follows then there is no "one-size-fits-all" answer about the degree to which your products and services have to be configurable. The key is to hit the marketplace sweet spot. This will help you thrive.

Notes:

....

....

....

....

....

64

Eliminating Friction In Configurable Products And Services

Is it all about your company--the product or service provider--or all about your customer?

If it's all about your company, watch out! Someone will come along who is better focused on the customer and take market share from you.

How can you tell if it's all about you?

There's friction in the marketplace between what your company offers and what your customers really want and expect from your company.

Friction will keep your company from thriving.

Notes:

....

....

....

....

....

....

65

Are Your Customers Getting What They Want And Need?

Increasingly, customers expect to be able to influence the products and services they buy.

For low-end consumer goods, e.g., food products, items you would tend to find at large retail chains, etc., mass-produced products meet the essential consumer need. However, there are niche product areas where the ability to tailor the end product is valued and appreciated.

For higher-end products and services, the provider must offer some degree of choice. The days of a "one-size-fits-all" solution satisfying market need are behind us. And, of course, the challenge for the providers becomes containing costs as variety increases.

Is there an enthusiasm gap between what you offer and what your customers expect and want? If there is an enthusiasm gap, it is incumbent that your organization to close the gap if you expect your organization to thrive.

Notes:

....

....

....

....

....

INNOVATION

66

What Are You Doing To Become The Tallest Tree?

On cold mornings here in Silicon Valley, birds flock to the top of the tallest tree to capture the earliest rays of sunlight to warm themselves after the winter night. They are not attracted to the shorter trees—they only want the tallest.

Isn't that the way of the marketplace? Don't some companies dominate their competitors to the point where the others are treated as a large mass of indistinguishable companies?

Apple dominates—the world can't wait to see what they are doing next. Netflix and video-on-demand are putting Blockbuster out of business. Amazon.com is the place where I buy books to the exclusion of other online resellers. How many of you flocked to Bing and abandoned Google?

What are you doing to become the tallest tree?

Notes:

. . . .

. . . .

. . . .

. . . .

. . . .

. . . .

Avoid
Follow-Ship

The Reuters headline reads: *"Google's Schmidt undaunted by Apple or Facebook."*

And, so Eric Schmidt should be. He believes in Google's standing in the world and is working hard to further enhance Google's position as an innovator. There is no reason to believe that Google won't continue to thrive in a sea of opportunity.

What is the lesson? Being an innovation leader is not about "follow-ship." Just ask the companies that thrive.

Notes:

....

....

....

....

....

....

Innovating Business Processes Creates Value

Business process innovation can be as value laden as product or service innovation.

The San Jose Fire Department just laid off 50 firefighters and will close a couple of fire stations due to budget constraints (and, frankly, the unwillingness of their unions to make concessions to save the jobs).

Sunnyvale, California, a major city in Silicon Valley, has an entirely different and revolutionary approach and, as a consequence, will lay off no one. Sunnyvale's Public Safety Department combines fire, police, and emergency medical services into one department. Those in police roles carry the equipment to take on firefighter roles at a moment's notice. Everyone is cross-trained to assume different roles. The officer in a police squad car this week might be stationed in a firehouse next week. Sunnyvale's lean approach drives great efficiency, agility, and cost-effectively leverages total resources.

What process innovation is your team or company ignoring that can change the game and help you thrive?

Notes:

....

....

....

....

69

Making
The Complex
Simple

When a company wants to talk to me about what they do, I really do not want them to be a solution in search of a problem. I want a company to understand my business challenges (or my client's business challenges), not merely talk about their technological capability.

I do not want them to make me think too much or too hard. I need to be able to "get it" very quickly, or I lose interest very quickly. Prospective customers are not much different.

Companies that thrive bring simplicity, not complexity, to their customer's world.

Notes:

. . . .

. . . .

. . . .

. . . .

. . . .

. . . .

70

Steve Jobs And Perfecting Solutions

Some of us get to make a more profound impact on our world than others. I'm thinking about you, Steve Jobs.

- When Steve Jobs announced the iPod, I scoffed at it. The iPod and iTunes transformed the world of music and how we distribute information. I missed it; Steve didn't.

- When Steve Jobs announced the iPhone, I scoffed at it. Did the world really need another smartphone? I missed it; Steve didn't.

- When Steve Jobs announced the iPad, I wondered what he had up his sleeve. He made the tablet computer worth owning. No other tablet device has come close to creating the excitement of the Apple tablet computer. I missed it; Steve didn't.

Steve Jobs has created a better world for his shareholders, his customers, and his employees. While Steve has not invented new things, he's perfected the Apple products offered in the marketplace. That has made Steve and Apple thrive.

What are you doing to perfect your offerings and your business execution to make your company thrive?

Notes:

....

....

....

....

The Global Impact Of Innovation

I shared a Fast Company Expert Blog post with a client that takes a look back at the office technology available during the NASA program to put a man on the moon back during the 1960's.

My client wondered on Twitter, *"When will another president have the guts to announce a 'man on the moon' project and what should it be?"*

I tweeted back, *"The project should be to eliminate US dependence on fossil fuels by 2030...an idea bigger than putting a man on the moon."*

My client tweeted back, *"...and probably with more impact on global peace ;)"*

Eliminating US dependence on fossil fuels (petroleum, coal, natural gas) will improve national security, create millions of jobs, reduce our carbon footprint, and help us thrive.

Isn't it time to tackle an innovation project like this?

Notes:

....

....

....

....

....

....

Eschewing Big Company Syndrome

Forbes.com had a interesting piece written by Steve Denning called *"Peggy Noonan on Steve Jobs and Why Big Companies Die."* Here is an excerpt:

> *There is an arresting moment in Walter Isaacson's biography of Steve Jobs in which Jobs speaks at length about his philosophy of business. He's at the end of his life and is summing things up. His mission, he says, was plain: to "build an enduring company where people were motivated to make great products."*
>
> *Then he turned to the rise and fall of various businesses. He has a theory about "why decline happens" at great companies: "The company does a great job, innovates and becomes a monopoly or close to it in some field, and then the quality of the product becomes less important. The company starts valuing the great salesman, because they're the ones who can move the needle on revenues." So salesmen are put in charge, and product engineers and designers feel demoted: Their efforts are no longer at the white-hot center of the company's daily life. They "turn off."*
>
> *IBM [IBM] and Xerox [XRX], Jobs said, faltered in precisely this way. The salesmen who led the companies were smart and eloquent, but "they didn't know anything about the product." In the end this can doom a great company, because what consumers want is good products.*

Is Steve on to something? Is he describing the cause of "big company syndrome?" Is this what keeps big companies from thriving?

Notes:

. . . .

. . . .

73

Error Correction Versus Innovation

If your company is overly focused on error correction, you simply wait until a problem occurs. Then, you correct the problem returning you to the same standard of performance you were at before the problem occurred. All the energy and attention expended resolving problems leaves you no better off than you were before the problem occurred.

If your company is concerned about raising the standard of performance, however, you must innovate.

Companies focus entirely too much on error correction and not enough on raising the standard of performance.

A relentless focus on innovation—product, service, and business process innovation—will ensure your company thrives.

Notes:

....

....

....

....

....

....

Simplifying Complexity Is Innovation At Its Best

I was invited to attend the Dell KACE Konference in San Francisco this past week, an event my spell-checker doesn't like very much. Here's my take-away:

Dell KACE is "the Apple" in its industry–addressing system administration problems with straight-forward, elegant, pragmatic technology solutions that customers crave.

The audience wasn't concerned about the veracity of new solutions being created–that seemed to be a given. Their concern was, "how soon will this be available?" If I had to assign a tag line to the development team, it would be something like, "We do the heavy lifting so you won't have to."

We live in a technologically complex world. Organizations that simplify complexity will thrive.

Notes:

....

....

....

....

....

....

Avoiding Death By Incrementalism

We make the world better when we simplify problems for customers when what we create is so glaringly obvious that people say to themselves, *"I wonder why nobody did that before?"*

We make things better when we step back, look carefully, and say, *"What exists can be done much, much better. What would be really exciting for our customers?"*

Steve Jobs didn't focus on incrementalism. He focused on what would excite and delight the world—what would create a compelling customer experience. And, did Steve and Apple ever succeed in creating excitement!

The technology world paused to pay attention whenever Steve took the stage—people couldn't wait to hear how he and Apple would rock their world.

- There were mp3 players before the iPod.
- There were smartphones before the iPhone.
- There were tablet computers before the iPad.

None of the forerunners to these Apple products comes close to capturing the excitement that Apple created. Not even close.

The lesson? Incrementalism won't help your company thrive. A relentless focus on the customer experience will help your company thrive.

Notes:

. . . .

. . . .

. . . .

76

Delighting And Exciting Customers Via Innovation

Innovation comes from the creation and implementation of customer-centric ideas that excite and delight. Innovation is about engaging and connecting with customers in the most direct, value-laden way possible, making them feel like they are the most important aspect of your company's life.

Do your customers feel as though it's all about your company or all about them? If it's the former, you've got some work to do!

Example: The Apple iPad--hardly the first tablet computer--transformed the marketplace and no tablet computer today is even close in terms of desirability. Not only is it a superior hardware design, the user interface, the supporting infrastructure of iTunes, and the manner in which newspapers and periodicals have been tailored to the iPad have created a superior customer experience.

The right innovations--whether it be via a product, service, or business application that allows your customers to interact with your company--will ensure your company thrives.

Notes:

....

....

....

....

....

Value Versus Cost

A good friend heard her services are "expensive" by way of third-parties who have never worked with her. Her clients sing her high praises while the folks who could benefit from her services flounder.

If a product or service delivers exceptional value far beyond the investment required to acquire the product or service, is it expensive? Certainly not.

Value comes from the outcomes that flow from money invested. If the resulting value is small, then the price might indeed be "expensive."

If the value is substantially greater than the investment required to gain the benefits of the product or service, is it expensive? No.

The people and companies that thrive base investment decisions on outputs or outcomes produced for money invested in products or services.

Notes:

....

....

....

....

....

....

78

Strategy Versus Execution

I've long been concerned about HP's CEO Mark Hurd being so focused on execution that he lost sight of the need to innovate to ensure a sustainable, viable business. Now, in light of Hurd's unplanned departure from HP, others are suddenly writing that it is time for an HP CEO who embraces the need to innovate.

The CEO's role is to create and deliver a compelling strategy. The COO's role is driving execution. HP does not have a COO, a structural problem in the company's leadership team that may have distracted Hurd. Hurd acted like an extremely effective COO, not a CEO.

Great strategy and great execution are required to ensure a company thrives.

Notes:

....

....

....

....

....

....

LEADERSHIP

The Role Of Excitement In Business

Do employees who are continually working through disruptions do their highest and best work for the organization and its customers? Certainly not!

In the business world, there is far too much emphasis on correcting disruptions—the things that aren't working for us or serving us well—and not enough emphasis on doing things that create excitement.

Leaders owe it to themselves and their teams to continually evolve their organizations to a future state focused around excitement. Excitement is uplifting for the entire organization and contributes to higher employee loyalty, higher customer loyalty, and reduced churn.

If there is no excitement, what is the point?

Notes:

....

....

....

....

....

....

A Leader Must Lead

I caught an interesting television episode of "Kitchen Nightmares" this week featuring Chef Ramsey, the Simon Cowell of the restaurant business. He was brought in to save a failing restaurant.

The owner made the mistake of thinking that the restaurant she had purchased 5 years earlier was a turn-key business that would require no additional thought, innovation, training, systems, quality control, etc. She demonstrated no passion for "making the business work"—she merely expected it to work as it had for the seventeen years prior to her acquiring it.

Merely showing up and going through the motions won't make any business thrive.

Notes:

....

....

....

....

....

....

Keys To Implementing Change

Implementing organizational and system change is (more often than not) fraught with peril. From the book Social Change 2.0: A Blueprint for Reinventing Our World comes this compelling insight:

People are willing to change if they have a compelling vision and are provided tools to help them bring it into being.

Have you articulated a compelling vision for change you are involved with? Have you provided the tools (money, resources, bandwidth, encouragement) to bring change into being?

Notes:

....

....

....

....

....

....

82

Be Intolerant Of A Bad Status Quo

I once knew of a brilliant, product development senior executive who used an expression that sticks with me to this day:

"Sometimes, when something is a little bit broken, it has to become dittle bit more broken before it can get fixed."

Why, when we know that things don't work or serve our needs, do we tolerate this state of brokenness?

Companies that thrive are intolerant of things that are broken and jump to correct the situation.

Notes:

....

....

....

....

....

....

83

Are There Really Unforeseen Circumstances In Business?

Sandwich board sign on the street outside an event:

"Psychic Fair canceled due to unforeseen circumstances"

Besides the obvious contradiction here, many "unforeseen" circumstances in business are foreseeable.

Companies that thrive pro-actively anticipate the "unforeseen" circumstances. You aren't tied to the railroad tracks, so don't behave as though you are. Ask for help!

Notes:

. . . .

. . . .

. . . .

. . . .

. . . .

. . . .

84

You Decide How And When Your Business Evolves

You have to decide where you want to take your business.

If you want to be timid, stop investing and wait for Wall Street to tell you everything is fine and it's okay to invest in your business again, you'll be too late for your competition will have stepped into the vacuum you created while you decided to ride out the storm in a safe harbor, positioning your competitors to leapfrog your market position.

This is the time when companies need to be investing in systems and processes, people, and new or enhanced products and services to be in the best position possible to thrive coming out of the economic downturn.

Notes:

....

....

....

....

....

....

What Leaders Can Learn From Jesuits

Silicon Valley recently lost one of its most successful former CEOs: Father Paul Locatelli, past President of Santa Clara University, a Jesuit university, and my alma mater. Our newest Pope—Pope Francis—is the first Jesuit to be named Pope. Look at the global excitement he is creating for Roman Catholics and non-Catholics alike.

John Baldoni introduced me to a book called "Heroic Leadership" subtitled *"Best Practices of a 450-Year Old Company That Changed the World"*, written by Chris Lowney, the story of what *"16th century priests can teach 21st-century sophisticates."* Chris writes:

"But the stereotype of top-down, immediate, all-transforming leadership is not the solution; it's the problem. If only those positioned to lead large teams are leaders, all the rest must be followers. And those labeled followers will inevitably act as followers, sapped of energy, and drive to seize their own leadership chances.

The Jesuit model explodes the 'one great man' model for the simple reason that everyone has influence, and everyone projects influence—good or bad, large or small—all the time. A leader seizes all of the available opportunities to influence and make an impact. Circumstances will present a few people with world-changing, defining moment opportunities; most will enjoy no such big-time opportunities in their lifetime. Still, leadership is not defined by the scale of the opportunity but by the quality of the response."

The notion that everyone is a leader can help your company thrive.

Notes:

. . . .

. . . .

86

Teams Can Become Too Comfortable

From Sir Richard Branson's book, Business Stripped Bare comes this insight:

> "...teams: they don't last forever. Think of a team as being like the cast in a theatrical play. Actors who work too long together on the same show for too long grow stale. When the business lets you, shake things up a little."

The status quo represents danger. Shaking things up a little will allow constant evolution and help your business thrive.

Notes:

....

....

....

....

....

....

Leaders Go To Where The Work Is

There is a Japanese concept that I know as "gemba" meaning, "go to where the work is." There are great lessons that can be learned "where the work is."

The TV show Undercover Boss captures CEOs going to where the work is. It is interesting watching the executive's eyes being opened to realities their employees face every day.

If more leaders would go to "where the work is," they would be adding value beyond belief and helping their employees and organizations thrive.

Notes:

....

....

....

....

....

....

88

Business Evolution Is A Continuous Journey

I attended the grand opening of Dell's Social Media Listening Command Center in Round Rock, Texas. Manish Mehta, Vice President for Social Media & Community, led the effort to create this critical function. The grand opening marks a significant milestone, so significant that Michael Dell and other key executives participated in the grand opening.

I asked Manish if this milestone was consistent with his vision. He responded, *"Yes, for version 1.0, but I have a vision out through 9.0."*

I love his answer. He pauses to celebrate this milestone, knowing that the journey is not complete. A long-term vision helps Manish and his team thrive.

Notes:

....

....

....

....

....

....

Leaders Are Honest With Their Teams

A leader tells people what they need to hear, not necessarily what they want to hear.

Do you want people saying, "nice idea" or "our company isn't where we need to be on this—we need to take action now!"

The path of least resistance is to "go with the flow." This is seldom the best path.

Companies that thrive welcome a different, stronger, more compelling perspective.

Notes:

. . . .

. . . .

. . . .

. . . .

. . . .

. . . .

90

You Can't Be Too Close To Customers

Karen Quintos, Chief Marketing Officer for Dell, encourages all professionals to spend time in customer service, getting closer to real customers and the issues they face. Karen believes that the perspective gained in customer service is invaluable as an individual's career evolves.

Getting closer to the customer will help you and your company thrive!

Notes:

....

....

....

....

....

....

Dwell On Possibility

There is a lot of noise in our world. There are too many prognostications about negative things in our lives. The media keeps us fixated on drama and trauma with respect to war, our economic standing in the world, our personal economic security, mankind's injustice to others, political infighting in our country, etc.

I saw a banner hanging in our church on Christmas Eve that bore a message worth pondering:

Dwell on Possibility

Dwelling on the possibility that we don't have to be at war, we don't have to worry about our economic standing in the world, we don't have to worry about our personal economic security, we don't have to dwell on mankind's injustice to others, and we don't have to dwell on political infighting brings hope for something quite different than the media wants us to focus on.

We don't have to idly sit back and accept a fate that is less than what we want. We aren't helpless—we aren't tied to the railroad tracks waiting for the next train to pull into the station.

Dwelling on possibility that your world can be what you want it to be will help you and your business thrive. Dwell on possibility.

Notes:

....

....

....

You Are Either Growing Or Dying

In biology, it is said that something is either growing or dying–there is no steady state. The same is true for companies and departments within companies.

Embracing the status quo is perilous. While the status quo feels comfortable, the comfort comes with a price.

The best corporations eschew the status quo and are continually on the lookout for opportunities to enhance their value-add and relationship with customers. That's what ensures their companies thrive.

Notes:

....

....

....

....

....

....

93

The First U.S. Chief Information Officer Challenged Status Quo

Earlier this year, I had the pleasure of hearing Vivek Kundra, the very first Chief Information Officer of the United States government, speak at Dell World 2011.

Kundra had a thought-provoking story to share of the need for innovative thinking and reinvention across the the U.S. government in terms of I.T. systems and solutions. *[Please read this fascinating story in my Forbes.com guest blog post here: https://www.forbes.com/sites/dell/2011/11/16/lessons-from-president-obamas-first-cio/#573d28595d0e]*

Michelle Bailey, Vice President at IDC, an industry analyst firm, offers *"Kundra is a great example of how the future CIO needs to set a strategy and change the people, not just the technology."*

Vivek Kundra asked the tough questions that needed to be asked and took action. What tough questions are you asking to help you and your company thrive?

Notes:

. . . .

. . . .

. . . .

. . . .

. . . .

. . . .

94

Carrot Or Stick?

In an Austin elevator this week, I overheard 2 gentlemen talking about a need for organizational change. One gentleman said, *"Well, if they don't go for the carrot, we'll just have to bring out the stick."*

I exited the elevator shaking my head. Did they really believe this is the best approach for achieving enduring change?

Enduring change is created by engaging with stakeholders—the people who have to live day in and out with the change—in a meaningful way that captures and incorporates their feedback and is responsive to their needs.

The carrot or stick may result in compliance but fails to help the people, department, or the company thrive.

Notes:

. . . .

. . . .

. . . .

. . . .

. . . .

. . . .

95

The Need To Delegate Trust

If control is held too closely at the top of an organization or team, there is a lack of trust undermining effective collaboration. It takes more than merely delegating tasks—trust must also be delegated.

Teams need to be allowed to make mistakes. If people are allowed to make mistakes, the quality of the deliberation and decision-making increases as people gain confidence that they truly are making decisions that will be acted upon. If people feel as though the decisions made in the course of collaborating aren't likely to stick, they feel that there's not much point to the collaboration, and it weakens future collaborative efforts.

Trust is a critical component of leadership and collaboration—understanding this will help you thrive.

Notes:

. . . .

. . . .

. . . .

. . . .

. . . .

. . . .

Fixing The Culture Of A Company

A colleague has been asked to take on an assignment to "fix the culture" of a company and was seeking advice about how to proceed with a proposal. I wondered, *"How do you fix a company's culture when culture is really a composite of many attributes?"*

Culture is homogenized from attitudes, beliefs, behaviors, business execution, actual and perceived standing in the marketplace, etc. You have to move the needle on the underlying aspects of culture to move the needle on culture.

Improve the behaviors, beliefs, behaviors, business execution, etc., and you change the culture—this will ensure your company thrives.

Notes:

....

....

....

....

....

....

Believing In Your Value-Add

My mentor—Alan Weiss—advises me to approach the world from the following mindset:

> *"I offer tremendous value, which improves people's performance and lives. I am remiss if I don't assertively attempt to bring that value to everyone who might benefit from it."*

What if all people shared that belief about their contributions and value-add? Wouldn't that help them and their businesses thrive?

Notes:

....

....

....

....

....

....

Dealing With A Chronic, Disruptive Influence

Years ago, I had an employee who was a chronic, disruptive influence on my team and other teams in the company. She was an angry, bitter person who brought darkness to every situation or individual she encountered.

I wrote her up, gave her very specific examples of the problems, and told her in no uncertain terms in face-to-face meetings and in writing that this had to stop immediately. I told her there would be a zero-tolerance policy regarding any future transgressions, which would result in her immediate termination.

I gave her a 0.001% chance of succeeding. She took what I told her to heart and, to her credit, changed. I never so much as had a hint of any negative behavior. I don't know why I got through to her. I suspect it was because no one had ever confronted her about how she terrorized people.

As a manager, if you fail to confront a problem, you are complicit. A team can't thrive with toxic people.

Notes:

....

....

....

....

....

Leading In A Turbulent Environment

Focus on the wrong things can be debilitating. Too many people are focused on matters they have no control over. If this were a good thing, I'd not be writing about it.

We don't have control over the stock market, what then banks are doing, what the government is doing, what's going on in the global economy, what our competitors are doing, etc.

What we do have control over is setting our own strategy and executing that strategy, irrespective of all the ambiguities that we are exposed to.

We have to manage our businesses. If that means we need to turn off the news so we can focus, then so be it.

We must set a specific course and follow it, not become a rudderless ship being tossed about in a turbulent sea. This is key to thriving.

Notes:

....

....

....

....

....

....

What's More Important? Strategy Or Execution?

What is more important? Strategy or execution?

A failed strategy can keep your company or department from thriving just as much as failed or poor execution. Both are essential to thrive in your marketplace.

More executives "leave for personal reasons" due to failed execution than bad strategy.

Do you have the right strategy? Is your execution on par with expectations? If you are concerned about either of these, are you taking appropriate corrective action?

Notes:

....

....

....

....

....

....

About Dave Gardner

Dave Gardner is a management consultant, speaker, blogger, and author based in Silicon Valley.

He's been in the front row for the birth and evolution of Silicon Valley, the innovation capital of the world. Since 1992, DaveGardner.biz has focused on accelerating growth through change.

His clients include large corporations such as Cisco, Dell, Applied Materials, Nanometrics, LSI Logic, FujiFilm, and several lesser-known start-ups and small to medium-size businesses.

Dave has held management and senior management positions in Engineering, Manufacturing, Sales, Marketing, and Customer Service, and Product Management in a variety of high-tech industries, in the pharmaceutical and biotechnology industry, capital equipment manufacturing and in the fire/rescue vehicle industry.

He holds a BA from San Jose State University and an MBA from Santa Clara University. He is a former member of the Leadership Board for the College of Arts and Sciences at Santa Clara University.

Dave is a member of the Society for the Advancement of Consulting (SAC). He is Board Approved by SAC in "Configurable Products and Services Strategy & Implementation." He's the author of *Mass Customization: An Enterprise-Wide Business Strategy*.

Dave has been inducted into the Million Dollar Consulting® Hall of Fame.

He has written for Fast Company as an Expert Blogger, Forbes, and is a member of Dell's Customer Advisory Panel.

Dave can be reached via his website: **davegardner.biz** or or via **Linkedin: https://www.linkedin.com/in/ gardnerdave/**

www.ingramcontent.com/pod-product-compliance
Lightning Source LLC
Chambersburg PA
CBHW021833170526
45157CB00007B/2785